I0841828

Policing Reimagined

City-2-City

Also by Terrence A. Perry

Healing Lives Matter

Coaching In The Game: Bring Your "A" Game

America's Awakening: Healing America's Collective Inner Child

Life Mastery Begins With Healing The Whole
In Your Soul

Personal Power and Social Responsibility In
America 2020: Mastery of Personal Power

My Message of Self Worth: I Am Good Enough

Reinventing Yourself: Invest In You

Is America Ready To Heal?
America: The Good, The Bad, and The Ugly Revealed

America's Awakening: The Movements, The Murders,
The Memories, The Message

Fighting for the Soul of America

Policing Reimagined

City-2-City

Terrence A. Perry

Table of Contents

Policing Reimagined

City-2-City

Chapter 1

Enough is Enough

To ensure the long term safety of our communities, we must look beyond the police. Racism, corruption and police brutality are common in police departments across America. So, why do we keep treating the police as if they are the one true path to community safety? A police-first approach to public safety fails to address the underlying causes of crime, while contributing to our statues as the most incarcerated country in the world, and one with incredibly high levels of police violence. Why don't we try something different? We are seeking a more effective, fiscally responsible way to keep our communities safe; one that intersects with our righteous outrage at police violence and mass incarceration.

Killings of black men take a toll on black male mental health. For many black men, viral videos featuring the killings of other black men can weigh heavy on the spirit. Watching the disturbing footage can impact the mental health of African American men...it's exhausting to think that you can be up next. Systemic racialized trauma... America's tragedy. Stop quoting Dr. King to black people, it means nothing when these murders by police keep happening to black men and women. If you're white, stop saying you're not racist. As white people, you have benefited from the structure of racism and therefore, inherently racist. If you're not actively ant-racist, you're racist. George Floyd's death is a clear symbol in 2020 of the oppressions of racism... white people with their feet on our necks suffocating us—enough is enough...Let the riots began!!!

Chapter 2

A Damaged Culture: Slave Patrols

The death of George Floyd at the hands of a white police officer sparked widespread outrage. Floyd's death at the knee of white police officer Derek Chauvin reflects the racist roots of American policing. Outrage over racial profiling and the killing of African-Americans by police officers and vigilantes has recently resurfaced following the video footage of Floyd's brutal death on May 25, 2020. Former police officer Derek Chauvin, charged with 2nd degree murder, for pressing his knee into Floyd's neck for over eight minutes, suffocating Floyd to death as he initially stated he couldn't breathe, caused pandemonium in the streets of America and abroad. There have been many precedents to the Ferguson, Missouri protest that ushered in the Black Lives Matter movement in 2014, and the riots of 1992 after the acquittal of police for beating Rodney King.

These issues of race, class, and crime are rooted in racism and in American policing, first planted centuries ago and have not yet been fully purged. Policing in southern slave holding states had roots in "Slave Patrol" made up of white volunteers empowered to use vigilante tactics to enforce laws related to slavery. Members of the Slave Patrol could forcefully enter anyone's home based on suspicion of sheltering people of color who had escaped bondage. In 1838, the city of Boston established the first American police force. America now has over 500,000 police officers and a total of 40,000 separate police forces nationwide. Improved policing is the order of the day, so transformation is now in progress.

Chapter 3

Slave Patrols and More On Early Policing

Policing in southern states had roots in what was called "Slave Patrols." Squadrons made up of white volunteers empowered to use vigilante tactics to enforce laws related to slavery. Slave patrols would locate and return slaves who had escaped, punish enslaved workers believed to have violated plantation rules.

Slave patrol arose in the south in the 1700's. By the time John Adams became the 2nd U.S. president, every state that had not abolished slavery had slave patrols. Slave patrols could forcefully enter anyone's home regardless of race, based on suspicions that they were sheltering people who had escaped bondage.

Centralized municipal police departments began to form in the early 19th century, beginning in Boston and soon cropping up in New York City, Philly, Chicago and elsewhere in American southern states. The first police forces were white, male and more focused on responding to disorder than crime. Officers were expected to control a dangerous underclass, which included African-Americans, immigrants and poor people. Police corruption and violence against people were common place during the 1900s. Controlling disorder, lack of adequate police training, lack of non-white officers, corruption and slave patrols are among the fore runners of modern day police brutality against African-Americans.

Slave patrol formerly dissolved after the Civil War ended, but little relief from racist government policies was seen. Jim Crow laws—black codes still restricted pay, voting rights, and limited travel rights.

Chapter 4

Understanding The Police Mentality

What makes a good police officer? Communication skills, compassion and empathy, integrity, negotiation skills, eagerness to learn and mental agility.

How stressful is it to be a police officer? Policing is a psychologically stressful work environment filled with danger, high demands, ambiguity in work encounters, human misery and exposure to death.

What does a cop do all day? Police officers are tasked with maintaining order and keeping communities safe. Most officers start out as "patrol officers.' Typical day-to-day duties include assisting in emergency scenes, responding to burglaries and monitoring the roadways and stopping cars that driving erratically or speeding.

How do police officers stay calm? Surviving verbal conflict training is a class whereas officers look at techniques in "verbal de-escalation" or tactics to make sure situations don't end up becoming violent. Cops must learn to remain calm, refrain from profanity, and above all, exercise empathy with everyone involved in a situation. In an age of video capabilities on cell phones, officers must be concerned about image. It means a lot when officers are involved in an encounter. Encounters can escalate at any time, officers must stay alert but calm, utilizing de-escalation techniques.

Chapter 5

What Is Police Burnout?

Emotional exhaustion that sat in after seven to twelve years of policing. Also police burnout is a syndrome of exhaustion and cynicism often present in cops and people who work in the social service field. Now, one of the long term effects of stress felt in police departments is professional exhaustion, commonly referred to as burnout. Some cops try to deal with long term stress by partially withdrawing and toning down their reactions. In the end, they became indifferent, detached from work, physically tired, depressed and cynical. Burnout resembles its cousin, depression. Oftentimes they hangout together. Officers must scale down and find stress management activities. Reduce time spent exposed to emotional or mentally stressful situations. Officers may have to change jobs and find some less stressful activity. Taking yearly breaks then coming back may decrease stress and emotional burnout. Usually with burnout, there's compassion fatigue. When an officer is not able to feel compassion for another human being, then we see cases like Derek Chauvin's knee on George Floyd's neck for eight minutes and forty six seconds. We see cases and cases of police brutality; shooting black people when it's not necessary. Of course racism and hate plays a large part in this unethical immoral behavior, yet no justice is served. Officers must pay attention to the warning signs; physically, mentally and emotionally.

Chapter 6

Things Your City Can Do
To Help End Police Brutality

Here are 10 things your city can do to help end police brutality:

1. Stop criminalizing everything
2. Stop using poor people/social class to fatten city budgets
3. Kick I.C.E. Out of your city
4. Treat addicts and the mentally ill like they need help; not jail
5. Make policy makers face their own racism
6. Ban racist policing
7. Obey the fourth amendment
8. Re-imagine safety and security in our communities
9. Involve communities in big decisions
10. Cities should stop over spending on policing

Police brutality or violence is legally defined as a civil rights violation where officers exercise undue or excessive force against a civilian.

Chapter 7

Holding Police Officers Accountable

A police department's policies and trainings are the basis upon which the reasonableness of an officer's conduct and therefore its legality and appropriateness will be determined in a disciplinary action or a criminal prosecution for excessive use-of-force or other misconduct. If the policy or training associated with the officer's conduct is too vague or permissive, even good cops can act like bad cops or bad apples, as they're being called. Thus, training and policy changes are essential components of an interconnected system of accountability. We have to know how to hold police departments accountable. Holding police officers accountable is perhaps the most difficult aspect of police reform due to opposition from "police unions" and traditional law and order advocates who have successfully campaigned for statutory barriers to accountability.

Abolishing "Qualified Immunity" is unlikely to alter police behavior. In practice, not theory, the courts shield officers by applying the doctrine aggressively to protect officers against lawsuits. The plaintiffs would have to point to other cases declaring essentially identical conduct unconstitutional, which is a difficult hurdle even when police conduct appears clearly to be wrong. Former Police Officer Derek Chauvin who murdered George Floyd may not be held liable by the courts if Mr. Floyd's lawyers are not able to point to an earlier case making clear that Derek Chauvin's actions of kneeling on a restrained person's neck for eight minutes was unconstitutional.

Chapter 8

Understanding the Communities You Serve

Police officers must understand and have knowledge about the communities where they work. A knowledge of the community and its people are required for informed public safety efforts. Proximity is key to building trust and it improves the ability of cops to keep people safe and it helps in the investigation and evaluation of crimes. Officers should live in the communities they serve. There should be an age and education requirement to be a police officer. Carrying a weapon with the authority to arrest and manage conflict requires skills and maturity. Many police departments hire police officers to serve at age 18 with just a high school diploma before they are legally eligible to drink or exercise the discretion we restrict to adults who are 21. A minimum age and minimum education requirement will improve officer safety and community safety.

The transfer to federal military equipment should end. Militarized police departments are significantly more likely to kill civilians. More than six billion dollars' worth of military equipment have been transferred to over 8,000 law enforcement agencies. Grenade launchers, military aircraft, machine guns, night vision goggles, etc. The Department of Defense's 1033 program need to be eliminated to mitigate damage to public trust in protecting community members. Congress must eliminate this section of the National Defense Authorization Act to prevent the transfer of military equipment.

Chapter 9

Why Is Police Reform So Difficult?

Why is police reform in the United states so difficult? Why can't the power-that-be see the implicit bias and racism in the police departments? The current president is minimizing and ignoring the serious foundational issues plaguing American policing, often use the term "bad apples" to describe police brutality and the misconduct of a "theoretical" "handful of officers." President Donald Trump's National Security Adviser flatly denied that there is systematic racism, claiming that a "few bad apples" were giving law enforcement a bad name. This is why police reform is so damn difficult, because the leaders reject the systemic root cause of the problem which is racism. Reform must focus on policing as a whole, and not limit the options to individual strategies such as trainings on "excessive use of force." The solutions to police reform have to be broader in scope and the approach has to be rooted in "meaningful accountability." A menu-of-options approach where as a handful of changes were adopted but other fundamental strategies are left out and that will not work effectively. Police reform must require and promote procedural justice and reduce implicit bias by having officers interact directly with community members. Also de-escalation policies and the duty to intervene when other officers engage in misconduct. Honestly, these procedures have been utilized as individual strategies, but did not work. A more "common based public safety model" is needed. Many of these reform strategies emerged after high profile killing in Ferguson, Missouri of Michael Brown, New York's Eric Garner and Cleveland's Tamir Rice by police officers.

Local government invested in body cameras, restrictions of miltary equipment by police department and expanding oversights of police actions through review boards. These strategies were based on research and had significant support from a range of experts, community leaders and police organizations. Training and policy changes were never designed to be the totality of police reforms. Other recommendations to training and education included building trust and legitimacy, policy and oversight, technology and social media, community policing, crime restrictions and officer wellness and safety training. Other reforms include independent investigations, prosecutions of police violence, limits to use of force and fair union contracts. All of these reforms are crucial to reforming policing and should not be discarded as unproven strategies. They provide instructions to police officers on their roles and responsibilities, how they should conduct themselves in different scenarios and ideally, the limits of their authority.

Chapter 10

Policing ReImagined

Improving public safety by building trust with communities and changing police culture requires authenticity and accountability. We need to fundamentally change the culture of policing to build trust, legitimacy and accountability. New laws should require disclosure of police violence. There are18,000 police departments in the U.S. and there is no federal law requiring departments to disclose when officers kill or severely injure citizens. Without data, the scope of police violence can't be accused.

Police violence directed at black people is a legacy of history of racial injustice. Police have long been the face of oppression—from tracking down fugitive slaves to allowing and participating in racial terror lynchings to beating non-violent civil rights demonstrators. The history of violence and racial oppression has allowed police officers to see themselves as agents of control, as soldiers trained in fighting, shooting and physically dominating their enemies. We need to create police departments where officers accept a role as guardians, with a commitment to protect and serve anyone; even the people they are arresting. Police officers are government agents who work for communities. There needs to be an obligation to reveal data about use-of-force, so there can be accountability. Congress must pass a federal law requiring disclosure.

Chapter 11

Police Officer Re-Training

The issue of <u>Use-of-Force:</u> a use of force standard and best practices should be updated and upgraded and recreated. The use-of-force by police officers has no universally agreed upon definition. The amount of effort required by police to compel compliance need not be.

<u>Choke Colds</u>: Bans on police use of choke holds and other neck restraints are finally being enforced. The choke hold technique has been a subject of controversy for many years.

<u>De-escalation of Situations:</u> Situational awareness is essential. Officers are trained to judge when a crisis requires the use-of-force to regain control of a situation.

<u>Police Misconduct:</u> inappropriate conduct or illegal actions taken by police officers in connection with their official duties: such as covered false confessions, false arrests, intimidation, false imprisonment, racial profiling, perjury, witness tampering, police brutality, corruption, etc.

<u>No Knock Policy changes:</u> Law enforcement entering into someone's property without prior notification of the residents is a policy requiring change. Law enforcement will enter after they identify themselves—Breaonna Taylor was killed in a no knock raid.

<u>Implementation</u>— No knock warrants conflict with the right of self-defense and stand-your-ground laws. No-knock warrants are prone to lead to deadly use-of-force by police and the death of innocent people. The no knock warrant is issued by a judge, and it allows cops to enter without knocking.

<u>De-certification</u>—a remedy for misconduct; revocation of a cop's license due to misconduct.

Abolish Qualified Immunity—It was designed to protect cops from law suits seeking money dames.

Chapter 12

Law Enforcement Is Not Above The Law!!!

In Augusta and Washington, lawmakers should take steps to address violations of the constitution by officers sworn to uphold the law. A police officer slammed a five foot tall mother to the ground in front of her children, causing her to lose consciousness. The court threw out her case against the officer before it could go to jury. An officer drove his SUV into the path of a fleeing motorcycle, killing the driver. The court tossed the case. Police officers fired at a family's dog, but instead shot a ten-year-old boy lying on the ground with five other children. The court dismissed the case. Again and again, officers have escaped legal accountability for their brutal violations of the constitution. Those violations disproportionately affect black people. This impunity is made possible by that legal doctrine we know as "Qualified Immunity." It protects victims of police brutality from obtaining justice under civil rights laws. "Qualified Immunity" allows courts to throw out any case against a police officer—even when the officers' actions are unconstitutional, unless there is another court findings that the officer violated the constitution by committing the same abuses in the same circumstances. Replica cases often doesn't exist precisely because earlier courts have done the same thing; tossing cases out based on "Qualified Immunity." Police officers are not above the law, and we must stop treating them like they are.

Chapter 13

Who Police the Police?

Law enforcement accountability is missing in the justice system. The supreme court could decide soon whether it will take a closer look at a legal doctrine it created nearly 40 years ago that critics say is shielding law enforcement and government officials from accountability. It protects an officers ability to make snap decisions during potentially dangerous situations. The legal doctrine known as "Qualified Immunity," arguing that it is not grounded in the proper legal authorities and too often shields officers from accountability. When the supreme court grants "Qualified Immunity," it sends a message to the people that their rights don't matter. Under the doctrine, an officer will not be liable even if he violates the constitution, unless it was "clearly established" by prior cases that his conduct was unconstitutional. That requires a high bar and makes it difficult to win unless the situation is similar to a prior case with nearly identical facts. In some cases with unique fact patterns, of which there are many, officers have been granted immunity even if they have been found to have acted in violation of the constitution. The cases before the court involving excessive force by the police have never been more relevant.

Chapter 14

Eliminating Qualified Immunity

"**Q**ualified Immunity" is designed to protect all but the plainly incompetent or those who knowingly violates the law. Law enforcement officers are entitled to "qualified immunity" when their actions do not violate a clearly established statutory or constitutional right. "Qualified Immunity" is a legal doctrine that protects government officials from law suits seeking money damages. The doctrine applies when officers are exercising discretion in their official capacity. The defense of 'Qualified Immunity" when invoked successfully, leads to dismissal of civil claims.

You have the right to sue the police if you are searched, arrested, or detained without a legal reason. If a police officer use more force than needed against you or took your property or damaged it or destroyed it without a legal reason, then the officer can be sued. Send your complaint by certified mail so the police cannot deny having received it. Also send copies to your local ACLU and NAACP chapters. You can make a formal complaint in writing to the chief of police and send a copy to Internal Affairs Divisions as well. Just remember, the officer, may use the defense of "Qualified Immunity" which clears the officer legally.

Chapter 15

Defund the Police

Advocates for defund the police movement argue that shifting funding to social services which can improve some things such as mental health, addiction and homelessness is a better use of tax payers money. This approach enhances the push to decriminalize and de-stigmatize people with mental health issues and addiction problems. Since the "overcriminalization" of people addicted to crack cocaine in the 1990's, some scholars and policy makers have said that this shift is long overdue. Police officers respond to everything from potholes in the street to cats stuck up in trees. Also, police officers are asked to complete lots of paper work and online forms. Documentation is important. It could be argued that reducing officers workload would increase their likelihood of solving violent crimes. Police officers are overworked and overly stressed. Focusing on mental tasks throughout the day is inefficient and a waste of tax payers money. Other government agents/agencies should be responsible for these and receive adequate funding for doing these services. Police officers are not that successful as people think at solving violent crimes, like rapes, robberies and aggravated assaults go uncleared. Police are being used more to control the movement of black people than for solving crimes. Stop and frisk should be unconstitutional.

Chapter 16

The Breathe Act is presented by the Electoral Justice Project of the movement for black lives. This visionary bill diverts our taxpayers dollars from brutal and discriminatory policing and invest in a new vision of public safety, a vision that answers the call to de-fund the police and allows communities to finally BREATHE free.

In honor of the lives of those stolen by the police and state—sanctioned violence—Breonna Taylor, Tony Mcdade, Natasha McKenna, George Floyd, Aiyana Stanley-Jones, Elijah McClain, Pearlie Golden, Kayla Moore, Freddie Gray, Atatiana Jefferson, Oscar Grant and far too many more... we are rising up against all the ways the criminal-legal system has harmed and failed to protect black communities. The current moment requires a solution that fundamentally shifts how we envision community-care and invest in our re-imagined America. History is clear that we cannot achieve genuine safety and liberation until we abandon police, prisons and all punishment paradigms. Mike Thompson and three co-sponsors officially introduced the BREATHE ACT into congress. Their efforts paid off on May 2, 2020. "We had an amazing day on Capitol Hill. The energy and excitement from our dedicated pact reps was clearly evident," said Anne Marie-Hummel, ARRC, Executive Director.

Chapter 17

The Justice In Policing Act of 2020

Congressional democrats rallied Monday around broad police reform legislation, urging President Trump and the republicans to rapidly embrace measures aimed at boosting law enforcement accountability, changing police practices and curbing racial profiling. On Wednesday, June 17, 2020, the senate unveiled their bill to reform the police. The proposal marks the latest efforts by lawmakers to overhaul U.S. law enforcement in the face of unrelenting pressure from activists in wake of George Floyd's death. The bill comes a day after President Trump signed executive order that would incentivize police departments to update their standards and practices as well as strengthen efforts to track officers misconduct. The Republican bill would incentivize enforcement agencies to "ban the use of choke holds" by tying the funding to whether departments have prohibited the practice, except when deadly force is authorized. Ramped up data collection efforts to track when an officer's use of force results in death or serious harm are enforced also.

Also, there is federal money provided for additional training on alternatives to the use of force. The bill also includes language recognizing the history of lynching in the United States. They have strengthened penalties for falsifying police reports, and they have sent the Attorney General reports on "No Knock Warrants."

A commission to study issues that affect black men and boys have been created as well. Unlike the democrat bill, the republicans bill does not address the issue of qualified immunity.

About the Author

Terrence A. Perry is a strategist and community change agent who helps people live and thrive, not just exist and survive. He has a BA in Psychology and is a certified life coach. Perry has been working in the human service field for over 30 years and continues to be an advocate for justice and equality. He utilizes his own knowledge and experience as well as the works and philosophies of T.D. Jakes, Carol Dweck, Jennifer Thomas and Gary Chapman, and many others to clearly and effectively explain his points views about America and what we need to do to heal.